HOWARD BOOKS
A Division of Simon & Schuster, Inc.

NEW YORK NASHVILLE LONDON TORONTO SYDNEY

Mary Mary

Erica Campbell *and* Tina Campbell

with Leigh McLeroy

be U

Be Honest,

Be Beautiful,

Be Intentional,

Be Strong,

Be You!

Published by Howard Books, a Division of Simon & Schuster, Inc.
1230 Avenue of the Americas, New York, NY 10020
www.howardpublishing.com

Be U © 2010 by Mary Mary

Library of Congress Cataloging-in-Publication Data

Mary Mary (Musical group).
  Be U: be honest, be beautiful, be intentional, be strong, be you! / Mary Mary, Erica Campbell and Tina Campbell.
        p. cm.
1. Spiritual life—Christianity. 2. Christian life.
3. Self-actualization (Psychology)—Religious aspects—Christianity.
I. Campbell, Erica. II. Campbell, Tina. III. Title. IV. Title: Be U.
BV4501.3.M2765 2010
248.4—dc22   2009030064

ISBN 978-1-4391-6071-8
ISBN 978-1-4391-7079-3 (ebook)

10 9 8 7 6 5 4 3 2 1

Cover design by Left Coast Design • Portland, OR
Interior design by Jaime Putorti
Cover photo by Bobby Quillard

*T*his book is dedicated to the teachers who were hard on us and required excellence. To our mom and dad, words cannot express how much you mean to us! Also, to our awesome siblings, pastors, and youth leaders, who taught us how to trust God. And to all the women who poured into us over the years, we love and appreciate you. To our loving and patient families, who understand the call on our lives; and the many pastors, bishops, and leaders who have allowed us to come and be ourselves in your churches, we are humbled. To everyone who will read this book, we pray that you are blessed, encouraged, and inspired to be all that God has called you to be! God, we just want to bring glory to your name.

Lovingly,

Erica and Tina

Contents

Acknowledgments

There are so many people who help to make this book possible, and we appreciate you more than you know. Managing all our travel schedules, deadlines, interviews, and edits has been crazy. But we thank God for you all and your skill and expertise you've brought to this project. To Dr. Holly Carter and Releve Entertainment, words cannot express the love and appreciation we have for you. Ebony MaGee, Megan Ashley King, we appreciate your hard work and your time. To Ricky Anderson our very capable attorney, thank you for dotting all I's and crossing all T's, we appreciate your expertise and protection. To Aja Johnson, who read the manuscript and gave us valuable input—from a teen's perspective. To Treiva Williams for an overnight edit.

To Philis Boultinghouse and Leigh McLeroy, we thank you for understanding our insane schedule and making this book come to life. We had a bit of a journey getting to this point, but I pray the lives changed and impacted for Christ will make it worth it for us all. Your passion for this project is overwhelming. We love you all.

Introduction

Your future is wide open! You can do anything, be anything, and accomplish everything your heart desires . . . if you believe. As sisters coming from a very large family, we believed in each other and put our trust in God. Growing up in Los Angeles wasn't always glitz and glamour. We had our challenges, our struggles, and definitely our disappointments, but those didn't define us.

We learned early on that faith in God was the substance of everything we'd ever hope for. For all the uncertainties of our younger years, he was our one sure thing. Neither of us would have made it far without him.

If you asked either of us today, "Who are you?" we wouldn't say "I'm singer Tina Campbell, half of Mary Mary," or "I'm singer Erica Campbell, the other half of Mary Mary." We wouldn't tell you about the awards we've received or talk about the people we've been privileged to know and work with, or even the amazing places we've been blessed enough to go. We'd say we're two sisters who love God and each other, who are blessed to be the wives of two wonderful men—Warryn S. Campbell II and Glendon Theodore Campbell—and the mothers of six amazing, precious children. We don't put our identity in what we do, even though we love what we do! We never have. Our identity rests solid in *whose we are*, and believe us when we say *we are God's*.

One of the hardest things about growing up is learning how to *be*. Your friends tell you to be one way. Your teachers or parents or others in authority tell you to be another way. The world tells you to be like the rich or famous or powerful people whose faces and stories are plastered everywhere. With all those people talking, it's tough to figure out who to listen to! The thing is, when you put all your effort into being somebody else, there's nobody being you!

God made you just the way you are. He put you in the family you're in, in the neighborhood you're in, the school you're in, and the skin you're in. He didn't make any mistakes; he wanted you to be you.

"Be you" is more than a slogan or a brand for us—it's a mission, flat out. We believe in it. We talk about it, tweet about it, write about it, sing about it. It keeps us focused on authenticity and truth, and keeps us honest: honest to God and honest with ourselves. Listen, nobody else is gonna be you like you. Trust that God knew what he was doing when he designed you. He made you for himself and gave you something the world needs that is yours alone to give. King David, from way back, said it like this:

> *For Thou didst form my inward parts; Thou didst weave me in my mother's womb. I will give thanks to Thee, for I am fearfully and wonderfully made; wonderful are Thy works, and my soul knows it very well. My frame was not hidden from*

Thee, when I was made in secret, and skillfully wrought in the depths of the earth. Thine eyes have seen my unformed substance; and in Thy book they were all written, the days that were ordained for me, when as yet there was not one of them. (Psalm 139:13–16)

So this book is for wonderfully-made you. And more than anything else, we hope it affirms the God in you, and points you to him. Then we hope it helps you see who he created you to be and encourages you to always be honest, be beautiful, be intentional, be strong, *be you*!

Erica and Tina

PART ONE

be *honest*

We're big on honesty. With each other. With our families

and our friends. And with the world. The Tina and Erica you

see on stage are the real Tina and Erica—not some manu-

factured image. We believe honesty is the way to go. Life

works better when you tell the truth, to yourself and to ev-

erybody else. Especially to God, 'cause he knows it all

anyway. You won't be fooling him!

See I decided that I cried

my last tear yesterday . . .

Yesterday I decided to put my trust in You.

—FROM "YESTERDAY"

Have mercy on me, O God, according

to your steadfast love; according

to your abundant mercy blot out my

transgressions.

Psalm 51:1 (ESV)

O N E

Yesterday

I will be merciful toward their iniquities, and I will
remember their sins no more.

HEBREWS 8:12

A Message from Erica

There are so many things in life we'd like to forget: bad hair days, bad
clothes, bad boyfriends, bad arguments, heartaches, and bad choices.
But what if we never experienced any hurt or regret, how would we
learn the life lessons we need to know? I've had my share of regrettable
yesterdays—but today I am grateful for a God who redeems my past
and restores my soul. I can't be held hostage by my yesterdays. I've
been set free.

I grew up loving the Lord, but I experienced a time when I was de-
liberately sinning and not following him as I should. (Can anybody
relate?) I believed one particular lie that a lot of girls believe—that the

love and acceptance I wanted could be found in a sexual connection with another person. If you're listening to that same story, the voice you're hearing belongs to the enemy and he is a liar. He always has been. He whispers that he's got what you want, that you're old enough, that you can handle it, and that what you do is nobody's business but your own. But he's lying.

What he *doesn't* tell you about—what nobody tells you about—is the guilt and sorrow that come from giving yourself away piece by piece. You don't hear the self-condemnation of someone who's betrayed their God and their own heart to get their way and meet their needs. So I'll tell you. It's painful. It can mess you up. There's no joy in it.

But I've got good news. If that kind of regret is a part of your "yesterday," God can make today a new day. If you understand him, you know that on the cross he paid for every mistake. Even the ones that you can't forget. Every sin and regret from yesterday is covered by his blood. Believe it. Accept it. His word says "There is therefore now *no condemnation* for those who are in Christ Jesus." That's no lie—that's the truth. He has the love you've been longing for—and it's a love that lasts.

You may be in church, serving God—choir, youth board, or whatever—but you're miserable because you're covering up yesterday's sin. You've got your church face on, but you don't have the joy of the Lord. But God has made a way out of yesterday for you and for me. It works like this: open up to him about your sin. Acknowledge it to him. Stop letting the enemy dangle your past over your head. He's killing you spiritually by keeping you isolated and alone. When he plays those old home movies reminding you of what you did in the past, you remind him of what *Jesus* did! Walk in God's forgiveness. Leave all your tears and regrets behind. They're so yesterday, and because of God's mercy, this is a new day.

be *U!*

Be certain that when God forgives, he forgets. You are forgiven, and your past cannot hold you captive. Be glad for today, and leave yesterday behind.

journal questions:

✽ What sins from your past drag you down with sorrow and regret?

_____

_____

_____

_____

_____

_____

_____

_____

_____

❋ Copy the verses in this entry in your journal, placing your name in them like this: "For I will be merciful toward _Erica's_ iniquities, and I will remember _Erica's_ sin no more."

_____

_____

_____

_____

_____

_____

_____

_____

✳ Write a letter to God confessing your "yesterdays" and thank him for not remembering or holding against you what he has forgiven.

_____

_____

_____

_____

_____

_____

_____

_____

_____

As far as the east is from the west, so far

does he remove our transgressions from us.

Psalm 103:12 (ESV)

There's no road that you can travel

to a place that's too far . . .

He's so close.

—FROM "SO CLOSE"

The Lord is near to all who call on him,

to all who call on him in truth.

Psalm 145:18 (NIV)

T W O

So Close

> For what great nation is there that has a god so near
> to it as the LORD our God is to us, whenever we call
> upon him?
>
> DEUTERONOMY 4:7 (ESV)

A Message from Erica

Do you know how close God is to you? He's so close he can hear you breathing—and so near he can wipe away your tears. God is so big that we imagine that he can't be near, but he's close . . . so close. Imagine your best friend, your tightest relationship. He's even closer still. He really is right there. Our own doubts and inadequacies trick us into believing he couldn't possibly be such an intimate friend, but he is always there. Always. Whatever you're going through, whatever emotion you're struggling with, you've got to press on to the point where the light comes on and you say "Oh, it's me that strayed—you're still here, God. You're just that close."

When I was younger I was dating a guy I thought I was going to marry, and one day it all just fell apart. I remember crying alone in my room, holding his picture, and saying, "Why, God, why did you do this to me? How could you let this happen?" Before long, my dad came in and sat next to me on the bed. I expected Tina to come, or my mom, or a girlfriend, but it was Dad who came in and said, "Don't worry, baby, it'll be fine. You'll see." That's just how near God wants to be to our pain and suffering. We look for friends, or a parent or teacher or pastor to step in—but it is our Father God who comes alongside and comforts us, because he's *that close*.

If you are crying out to him and you don't sense his presence or see your prayers being answered, maybe you're battling a "language barrier." Why not try and speak *his* language for a change? Speak the words of the Bible—his book—back to him. Say, "God, remember when you . . ." and then fill in the blank with something God has already said or done. Then make your request known to him. Tell him you're going to take a line from his manuscript, a promise he's made, a truth he's proclaimed, and give it back to him in his language. He's already promised he will never leave you or forsake you. He's not going anywhere. You have to realize that he's right there—and that his presence is not contingent upon your behavior, good or bad.

Listen, life happens. It's not gonna be sunshiny every day! But he knows what you'll go through, and he'll be with you. How can we gain strength if we haven't gone through trouble and trusted him to bring us out? Nobody grows and advances without trouble. Nobody. Those difficult moments are sure to come, but you'll make it through. Because he's right there. You watch. You wait. You'll see.

be *U!*

Believe that God is close to you in every circumstance, every trial, every joy. Be glad you have a God who is nearby and never far away.

journal questions:

❋ Does God seem near to you right now, or far away?

_____

_____

_____

_____

_____

_____

11

✳ Who is your closest friend? Who comes when you're hurt or confused or in pain? Do you believe that God is even closer than that friend? Why or why not?

_____

_____

_____

_____

_____

_____

_____

✳ Do you believe that God is only close when your behavior is good?

_____

_____

_____

_____

_____

_____

_____

_____

＊ How can God's nearness give you confidence when you face hard times?

_____

_____

_____

_____

_____

_____

_____

A man of many companions may come to ruin, but there

is a friend who sticks closer than a brother.

Proverbs 18:24 (NIV)

I should know by now there's no way,

no how, I could live my life without you.

—FROM "I TRY"

You have said "Seek my face."

My heart says to you, "Your face, LORD,

do I seek."

Psalm 27:8 (ESV)

T H R E E

I Try

The LORD your God is in your midst, a mighty one
who will save . . . he will quiet you by his love; he will
exult over you with loud singing.

ZEPHANIAH 3:17 (ESV)

A Message from Tina

Most of us try to get it right. We really do. We try to do our best, put first things first, take care of our families, love our friends. We try . . . but sometimes we fail. When we do, we don't need to beat ourselves up, or blame anyone else. We just need to understand that no matter how hard we try—we still need God to make life work. It's that simple.

The song says "I realize that I need your help, 'cause I can't make it all by myself." Sometimes I get the nagging feeling that I've let God down, and that I should be farther along in my faith. I'll think, "Why am I doing this? Why am I still letting the same old things trip me up?" But faith, in God's timing, always brings forth fruit. So when I get discouraged, when I struggle, it's a reminder that I can't make it without God. I try, but without him, I won't last long. I've got to go to my knees, because that's where my strength comes from.

Being a wife, a mother, a singer, and a businesswoman, life can get a little out of control. But when it does, I know I need more of God, not more of me. Nighttime is usually the best time for me to spend time with God, but some nights I get home late, or sleep overcomes me. And when I want to sleep in, or talk to God in the morning, that's when the baby wants to wake up early. Yet when you want something badly enough, you're willing to make the sacrifices required to get it. And I want more of God. He's the one that will get me where I need to go, and make me what I need to be. I need him more than I need extra sleep, or activity, or organization, or effort.

When I stop, drop, and do time with him, life flows better. With him, I'm able to manage the craziness, and take the challenges in stride. I can try and try and try on my own power, my own steam, but when I've connected with him, I'm able to do things differently—and do them better. My number-one need is time with God. There's nothing more important than that—because no matter how hard Tina tries, Tina will still fail. But when I put my life in God's hands, he looks beyond my faults and gives me another chance. I need him that much—and you do, too.

be *U!*

Be diligent to make time for God, no matter how busy your days become. He is always there, waiting for you. Before you are anything else, be his.

journal questions:

✳ What things do you try to do without God? Do you often succeed?

_____

_____

_____

_____

_____

_____

_____

_____

_____

_____

_____

_____

_____

✱ Are there things that compete for your time and attention at the expense of spending time with God? What are they?

_____

_____

_____

_____

_____

_____

_____

✱ Are there things in your past you wish you could undo?

_____

_____

_____

_____

_____

※ How often do you talk to your best friend versus God?

Draw near to God, and he will draw near to you.

James 4:8 (ESV)

God has smiled on me,

he has been good to me.

—FROM "GOD HAS SMILED ON ME"

The LORD will keep your going out

and your coming in from this time

forth and forevermore.

Psalm 121:8 (ESV)

FOUR

God Has Smiled on Me

> Are not two sparrows sold for a penny? And not one
> of them will fall to the ground apart from your Father.
> But even the hairs of your head are all numbered.
> Fear not, therefore; you are of more value than many
> sparrows.
>
> MATTHEW 10:29–31 (ESV)

A Message from Erica

Some people live a charmed life. They seem to get everything they want. Other people are *blessed.* They may not get everything they want, but they know what they do have comes from God and they give him the credit and thanks for it. It's one thing to trace our steps and say "This is how I got here"—but it's another thing to realize that the good things in our lives are *nothing* but the favor of God. They're not a result of what *we've* done, but of what *he's* done for us.

Growing up in Inglewood, California, we didn't live in the best neighborhood. There were gangs. We heard a stray gunshot now and then, and drugs were pretty common. But God chose to protect our family and to keep us. We never slept on the street. We were never hungry. There was a lot of love in our home, and in our church. We were prayed for. My mom used to do what we called "pray-bys." You've heard of drive-bys, right? Well, my mom had a different idea. She would walk into our rooms at night, stop over our beds, and pray. She'd ask God to protect us from harm, keep us from evil, and keep us safe. Tina and I say that's why we didn't sneak out at night: you never knew when a pray-by was coming, and when it did, you'd better be there!

I believe God answered my mom's prayers, too.

One Christmas the house we were living in caught fire. We'd been at church all day and got home in the evening around 10 p.m. When we did, we smelled smoke. We couldn't see anything burning—but my mom was convinced that we should not stay there. We went to a nearby relative's house to spend the night, and at 3 a.m. the phone rang. It was a neighbor telling us our house was on fire! A smoldering fire had ignited, and the floor caught fire in front of my baby sister's room. If we had stayed in the house, we might not have been able to cross the threshold and rescue her—and the house had security bars on the windows! I'm convinced God led my mom out of the house that night. God smiled on us.

A few years later when Tina was attending college, she was rushing to school and the brakes went out on her car. She landed upside down and facing the wrong way on an L.A. freeway—not a good place to be! But even though the car was totaled—every window busted out—Tina crawled out scratch-free. God smiled on her.

My mom and dad were not always together as we grew up. Sometimes dad was in our home. Sometimes he wasn't. But even though my parents' marriage was not rock solid, we knew we were loved. The world might say we came from a broken home, and by the world's standards, maybe we did. But even in the uncertainty of whether Mom and Dad would make it, God smiled on us. It doesn't mean our life was perfection, that we got a free pass, that everything was always great. But we knew for certain that no matter what trouble came our way, almighty God had our back. That's why I smile when I sing "God Has Smiled on Me."

be U!

There's nothing like experiencing the grace of God for yourself. Be attentive to the blessings in your life, so you'll know when God has smiled on you.

journal questions:

✳ Describe a time when you felt God smiling on you. What was happening? Who was there? How did you feel at the time?

_____

_____

_____

_____

_____

_____

_____

✳ Do you consider yourself blessed? Why or why not?

_____

_____

_____

_____

_____

_____

_____

_____

✳ In your own words, what is compassion? Are you a compassionate person? Do you believe God is a compassionate God?

_____

_____

_____

_____

_____

_____

_____

As a father shows compassion to his children, so the

LORD shows compassion to those who fear him.

Psalm 103:13 (ESV)

He's the biggest greatest thing,

the biggest greatest thing

I've never seen.

—FROM "BIGGEST, GREATEST THING"

I know that you can do all things;

no plan of yours can be thwarted.

Job 42:2 (NIV)

FIVE

Biggest, Greatest Thing

Holy, Holy, Holy is the Lord of hosts, the whole earth
is full of his glory.

ISAIAH 6:3 (NASB)

A Message from Erica

It's easy to look around and see all that God has made, but harder to
see the God behind it all. He really *is* the biggest, greatest thing in life:
bigger than the sky, higher than the mountains and the trees, wider
than the widest river and deeper than the oceans. He's that big. Sometimes I'm amazed that the God who made everything that is made us,
too. And he made us not to be victims, but conquerors. In fact, you
and I were created to have dominion over this great big world! Even
though at times we let the world "run" us, that's not the way it's sup-
posed to be. With him loving and leading us, we're meant to have a
bigger impact on the world than the world has on us.

It all starts with acknowledging that there is a great and mighty one who loves, cares, keeps, protects, and comforts us. How great is our God? He's so great that one day every living thing on the planet will worship him, and him alone. One day the skeptics' mouths will be shut and all the naysayers will see that our God is indeed an awesome God.

You may think that you're not much of a conqueror—that there's not much about this world that you can change. But you can control your attitude, even if you can't control your atmosphere. You can decide that depression will not run rampant in your mind. You can decide that anger will not rule your heart. You can decide to praise God in any situation—not because you're happy, but because he's good. Your perception will determine the quality of your reality *every time.*

For me, acknowledging that God is the biggest, greatest thing is very comforting. It keeps me levelheaded. When everything around me is chaotic, I ask myself, "Does God have it, or does he not? Is he bigger than anything that might happen? Do I believe it, or not?" And if I believe it, I'm not gonna despair. I'm not gonna let chaos rule. There are few things that I say that God never says. He never says "Uh-oh." He never says, "How can I possibly fix this?" He never says, "Oh. I didn't expect *that.*" And he never says, "I don't know what to do."

A few years back, when my daughter was about two, I was over-whelmed by something, and was crying in my room. She came in and just said, "I love you, Mommy." When she left I stopped crying, and re-membered the scripture that says God won't give us more than we can bear. Then I prayed and asked him to give me more of his perspective, more of his wisdom, and more of his peace. And pretty soon, I believed I could go through whatever might come with the "biggest greatest thing" in my corner.

be *U!*

If God is not the biggest, greatest thing in your life, then your picture of God is way too small! Be diligent to see God's power and strength at work every day, and when you do—and you will—give him some praise!

journal questions:

✻ Do you count God as the "biggest greatest thing" in your life?

_____

_____

_____

_____

_____

_____

_____

_____

✳ What things compete with him for that spot?

_____

_____

_____

_____

_____

_____

✳ Where do you see God when you look around? Can you see his greatness and power in his created world?

_____

_____

_____

_____

_____

_____

_____

_____

_____

_____

Therefore God has highly exalted him and bestowed on

him the name that is above every name, so that at the

name of Jesus every knee should bow, in heaven and on

earth and under the earth, and every tongue confess

that Jesus Christ is Lord, to the glory of God the Father.

Philippians 2:9—11 (ESV)

31

PART TWO

be *beautiful*

Not the way the world measures beauty . . . but on the inside, where it really counts. A woman who fears and trusts her maker is a beautiful woman. She knows what's going to last and what's worth striving for. She blesses others and isn't just out for herself. That kind of beauty isn't about your clothes or your hair or your jean size. It's about loving and living well. The kind of beauty that never fades.

It doesn't matter, whatever,

whenever I will, 'cause I love

you that much. . . .

—FROM "I LOVE YOU THAT MUCH"

God demonstrates his own love toward us,

in that while we were yet sinners,

Christ died for us.

Romans 5:8 (NASB)

SIX

I Love You That Much

> A new commandment I give to you, that you love one
> another, even as I have loved you, that you also love
> one another. By this all men will know that you are
> My disciples, if you have love for one another.
>
> JOHN 13:34–35 (NASB)

A Message from Erica

How committed are you to God? Are you gonna follow him only as long as he gives you what you ask him for? What if you don't get your way? Do you love him enough to sacrifice? Do you love him enough to wait? It's not easy to really, really follow God. We can give him lip service—sure. But real love always involves trust. Always. When you love somebody, you trust them. You believe in them. I love my husband. I trust him. I believe the best about him. Do you love God enough to trust him, and believe he's got your best interest at heart?

Do you believe he can change your circumstances, or help your insecurities? Do you believe he can transform the way you think and respond? Maybe you live in an abusive home where you're sad or afraid a lot of the time. Can you put it in his hands? If you love him enough, you will believe that he's got your back, and that he can change your environment, or keep you safe in it. Maybe you're being tempted to do something you know is wrong, and you can sense God telling you no. Do you love him enough to do what he asks, and to trust him?

That kind of trusting, believing love comes from one place. It comes from time spent together. The people I trust most are people I've seen in every kind of situation. I know how they'll respond, because they've already shown me. I know they'll be true because that's the way they've always been. It's the same with God. When you spend time with him, you come to know him better. And when you come to know him better, you trust him more. You learn to hear him when he speaks to you. When he says "Go here," you go. When he says "Say this," you say it. When he says "Do this," you do it. Sure, you may hesitate sometimes. You may try to talk yourself out of obeying by making excuses. But saying "I don't have time" or "I don't know enough" or "That's out of my way" just doesn't cut it when you know you've heard God speak. When the God you love and trust asks you to obey him, the question isn't "Is it convenient?" The question is, "Do I love him that much?"

be  U!

Be ready to love. Love is a powerful, powerful force in a world that's hungry for it. Show your love for God by loving others unselfishly.

journal questions:

✳ Have you ever been challenged to prove your love? How far would you go to show a friend or family member how much you care?

_____

_____

_____

_____

_____

_____

_____

_____

✳ Jesus' challenge to his followers was to love others the way he loved them. What kind of things did Jesus do for his friends?

_____

_____

_____

_____

_____

_____

_____

_____

✳ Is there anything in your life that you're holding back from God? Anything about which you'd say "This is mine, and I won't let you have it"?

_____

_____

_____

_____

_____

_____

_____

_____

_____

_____

_____

_____

_____

We love, because he first loved us.

1 John 4:19 (NASB)

Little girl, God made you so beautiful . . .

You formed my inward parts;

you wove me in my mother's womb.

I will give thanks to you, for I am fearfully

and wonderfully made; wonderful are your

works, and my soul knows it very well.

Psalm 139:13—14 (NASB)

SEVEN

Little Girl

> Charm is deceitful and beauty is vain, but a woman
> who fears the LORD, she shall be praised.
>
> PROVERBS 31:30 (NASB)

A Message from Erica

I spent most of my time as a little girl wishing I could be just one year older. (Funny how a girl's wishes can change!) I wished for other stuff, too. I wished I was a little cuter, and a little more popular. I wished I was more outgoing, and not so quiet and shy. I wished my parents had just a little bit more money, and I didn't have to wear quite so many hand-me-downs. I wasn't so different from most girls my age in my wishing, either.

Whether you're the popular girl or the studious chick, the rich kid or the poor one, you've probably wished for your share of things, too. Things like acceptance, love, approval, and security. Sometimes we have those things already—we just can't see them. As for me, I had great friends, a family who loved me, the talent to sing, and a place to do it. But the enemy tricked me into believing I had next to nothing!

I would look in the mirror and see my flaws, never realizing that God made me just the way he wanted me to be, and loved me exactly as I was! He had a perfect plan for me, but it took a while for me to accept and embrace it. Thank God we're born "little" and have the opportunity to grow into adulthood—if not, adulthood might be a complete disaster!

Now when I see a young girl who's unsure of herself or insecure in her looks or her gifts or her popularity, my heart goes out to her. I wanna say, "Little girl, you are so special just the way you are! There's no one in the world quite like you. God made you perfectly, according to his design, and he doesn't make mistakes." Girls struggle with confidence, and tend to look to their peers or boys for affirmation that they're okay. But that's the wrong place to look—and the mirror's no better. We need to look for affirmation and love and acceptance in God and nowhere else—and to be so sure of him that we're not insecure about anything else.

When we know we're loved, we're confident, and when we're confident, we're beautiful. So when you look in the mirror today, tell the little girl you see that she's just who God intended her to be—and don't waste another minute wishing to be anyone else!

be *U!*

Don't wish for anyone else's hair or hips or eyes—and especially not for anyone else's heart! Be the girl God made: unique, wonderful, you—precious in his sight!

journal questions:

✳ What do you see when you look in the mirror?

_____

_____

_____

_____

_____

_____

_____

_____

_____

✳ Are you happy with the way God made you? Why or why not?

_____

_____

_____

_____

_____

_____

_____

✳ Do you believe that you are "just the way God intended you to be"? Why or why not?

_____

_____

_____

_____

_____

✳ You are fearfully and wonderfully made. Thank God for making you just the way you are.

I have loved you with an everlasting love;

Therefore I have drawn you with lovingkindness.

Jeremiah 31:3 (NASB)

Lord, I'm thankful for my blessings,

everything that you gave . . .

—FROM "THANKFUL"

The LORD is my strength and my shield;

My heart trusts in him, and I am helped;

Therefore my heart exults,

And with my song I shall thank him.

Psalm 28:7 (NASB)

Thankful

> Be anxious for nothing, but in everything by prayer and supplication with thanksgiving let your requests be made known to God. And the peace of God, which surpasses all comprehension, will guard your hearts and your minds in Christ Jesus.
>
> PHILIPPIANS 4:6–7 (NASB)

A Message from Tina

For some reason, this song makes me think of air—who gives it, and who gets it. Just think about it: God gives the very air that keeps life in my body every day! If he didn't do anything else but give me the air that I breathe, that would be enough to keep me thankful until I took my last breath. Anything and everything else would be extra—a bonus.

If you're like me, though, you've got some expectations of God that go way beyond air. You're saying "Give me this," or "Help me with that," or "Fix this," or "Bless me in this way." You've got a list of things that God oughta do, right? But without the basics—without air—none of it would matter. He's the one that keeps you breathing in and out, even when you don't consider those breaths to be important. Without just that simple gift of air, we'd be in bad shape!

Although I want a whole lot more, I'm thankful for the air I breathe, and extra thankful for everything else. Because you never know what you've got until it's gone. Whether it's a friend who moves away, an opportunity you let pass, a sibling going off to college, a breakup, or even the death of a loved one, you don't really appreciate the value of a thing until it's gone.

That's why the time to be thankful is today. The moment for gratitude is this one, right now. So spend some more time laughing and singing and enjoying every gift *today*. Say thank you to God for everything—and I mean *every little thing*. No gift is too small to appreciate, and no time is better than now to say so.

You might think that "thank you" is optional, but I can tell you it is not. And it's not just about being polite. Gratitude changes your heart and changes mine—and it opens our eyes to even more blessings every time we practice it. So I challenge you: don't let a day go by without giving thankfulness a workout. Be deliberate in seeing God's blessings, and in giving him thanks. Then spread the thankfulness around to the others in your life: parents, siblings, friends, teachers, neighbors, co-workers—you get the idea, right? Just smile and say, "You didn't have to do it but I'm glad you did!" and see if you don't feel lighter than air when you do!

be U!

Gratitude is a beautiful thing. Remember to show it often. Be grateful and gracious to the givers in your life, and especially to God, who's the giver of every good and perfect gift!

journal questions:

✳ Count your blessings. Really. Make a list of all the good things God has given you, and keep adding to it every day.

_____

_____

_____

_____

_____

_____

✳ Is there someone in your life whose generosity has helped you grow? How could you creatively express your thanks to that person?

_____

_____

_____

_____

_____

_____

✳ When was the last time you said "Thank you"? Who did you say it to? What was the reason for your gratitude?

_____

_____

_____

_____

_____

✳ How often is thanksgiving a part of your prayers? Are you doing more asking than thanking?

_____

_____

_____

_____

_____

_____

_____

_____

As you have received Christ Jesus the Lord, so walk in

him, having been firmly rooted *and now* being built up

in him and established in your faith, just as you were

instructed, *and* overflowing with gratitude.

Colossians 2:6—7 (NASB)

PART THREE

be *intentional*

Don't be someone who just lets life happen to you and blames others when things don't go your way. Decide what matters most to you, get up, and pursue it. Go after your dreams. Work hard. Even when you can't change your circumstances, you can change your attitude. You and God together can make something beautiful of your life. When you move out, just make sure you're following him!

What do I gotta do to make you understand,

that I want what's best for

you and I always have?

—FROM "STAND STILL"

Stand firm and you will see the deliverance

the LORD will bring you today.

Exodus 14:13 (NIV)

Stand Still

He lifted me out of the slimy pit, out of the mud and mire; he set my feet on a rock and gave me a firm place to stand.

PSALM 40:2 (NIV)

A Message from Tina

"Stand still" sounds like strange advice in our day, doesn't it? But "stand still" is not a command to do nothing with your life—it's a wise instruction to wait for God's leading and guidance, to wait to hear his voice before you move out ahead of him. When I was less spiritually minded than I am today, I would make up my mind to do a thing, and then ask God to bless my plan. Plan A, plan B—whatever—I'd tell God my idea of how my life should go, and then ask him to join me and make it good.

Maybe you *have* "stood still," but didn't get the word you were waiting for. Sometimes the direction we seek doesn't come when we want it, or if it does, it doesn't line up with our plans. Guess what? God's not on the "You decide, I'll bless it" plan. Maybe he's not speaking because our requests (or demands?) don't line up with *his* plan. If you're asking the wrong question, it's hard to get the right answer. "Can I marry this person who's already married?" Not a good question. "Can I take this even though it belongs to somebody else?" Also not a good question.

Sometimes God's answer for us is "wait." Just wait. We mistake "wait" for no answer, but wait *is* an answer! Maybe he's saying "wait" because he knows if he gave a quick answer we would leave him, get lazy, get high and mighty, or abuse power. Or maybe we're just not ready for that promotion, that relationship, that gift we long for. We've got to wait to hear his voice. Right now my family is outgrowing our house. I'm ready to move. I'm thinking, "God, all the time I can give you is three months, 'cause I've got deadlines!" You know what? It could be that God means for us to stay crunched up because he wants to give us peace in the middle of chaos! Could be that God is trying to teach me by *not* moving us yet.

If we all made a greater effort to stand still, wait, and try to hear what God is saying, we could avoid some of the trouble, hassles, and headaches we experience. Do all you can do without getting ahead of him, and then say, "God—this is up to you. And I'm not movin' another inch until I hear from you." Mean it. Wait for him. Seek him. Stand still and watch your great big God move on your behalf!

be U!

Be content to stand still and wait for God to act on your behalf. He is faithful, and will never forsake his own.

journal questions:

✳ Are you moving too fast? Do you need to slow down and wait for God?

_____

_____

_____

_____

_____

_____

_____

_____

_____

_____

✳ Is there an area where you *are* waiting for God, but not hearing an answer? Are you asking him the right questions?

_____

_____

_____

_____

_____

_____

_____

✳ Can you think of a time when you waited, and God's answer wasn't what you hoped to hear? Can you see now how his answer was better for you?

_____

_____

_____

_____

✳ Is it hard for you to "stand still"? Why or why not?

So then . . . stand firm and hold to the teachings we

passed on to you, whether by word of mouth or by letter.

2 Thessalonians 2:15 (NIV)

While you've got a chance,

you oughta get up and give

God all you can. . . .

—FROM "REAL PARTY"

Rejoice in the Lord always;

again I will say, rejoice!

Philippians 4:4 (NASB)

TEN

Real Party

> Shout joyfully to God, all the earth; sing the glory of
> his name; make his praise glorious.
>
> PSALM 66:1–2 (NASB)

A Message from Tina

Have you ever attended a big game or a great concert, and been up and on your feet with thousands of other people, whooping and shouting and dancing like crazy? When everyone sings that certain song at the same time, it's bananas, right?

When our producer Warryn first brought us this song, I didn't really get it. I said, "What's the 'real party' all about?" He said, "Don't over think it, Tina—just listen." So I did, and he was right. There's nothing particularly personal or deeply spiritual about this song—just the determination to give God the praise he deserves without knowing the why's or the how's. When we praise him in spite of what's going on in our lives, not because we're on easy street but just because he's God—that's when we get the victory!

Sometimes you just need to give a shout of praise, lift up your hands, and tell God thank you. Nothing else matters in those moments, because we're doing what we were made to do—give glory to the God who loves us. So don't complicate or second-guess the praise when it comes. Let a phrase or a word or a verse stir you, and get lost in it. Say it over and over. Celebrate! Your life may not be perfect. You may even be in the middle of some serious pain or sorrow—but nothing in this life compares to the truth that the one who keeps this world turning every day gave his only son just for you!

I don't know about you, but when I feel loved, I feel happy. I want to sing, dance, jump, shout, and tell the world about it! Now that may not be a party in the sense that some know it. No club, no DJ, no pressure to put on my freshest clothes so everybody can learn how to dress just by checkin' my fresh—just my own personal, daily celebration of my God's love for me. I'm singing loud and maybe even off-key—but it doesn't matter how it sounds because there's nobody on my mind but God and me.

Just look around you: everything you see, he made. Every person you meet, he created. Every gift you've received, it's from him. He made all this so we could look up to him and say "Thank you. You're fantastic, God. I'm so grateful. I love you." When we forget ourselves and focus on him, everything else falls into place. When me and God get it crackin'—that's the real party!

be *U!*

David, the king of Israel, danced with joy before the ark of the Lord. Sometimes you've just gotta dance! Be ready to praise God with everything you've got when it's time to celebrate his goodness!

journal questions:

✱ Think of the biggest party you've ever attended. What were you celebrating? Was the celebration worthy of the occasion?

_____

_____

_____

_____

_____

_____

_____

_____

_____

_____

✳ Has anything ever made you shout with joy? If so, what?

_____

_____

_____

_____

_____

_____

✳ Think about a time you felt loved and happy—totally content. What did you do to "celebrate"?

_____

_____

_____

_____

_____

_____

_____

_____

_____

_____

_____

There is an appointed time for everything.

And there is a time for every event under heaven . . .

A time to weep and a time to laugh;

A time to mourn and a time to dance.

Ecclesiastes 3:1, 4

I need a solution,

and walking just won't get it.

—FROM "I'M RUNNING"

Do you not know that in a race all the

runners run, but only one gets the prize?

Run in such a way as to get the prize.

1 Corinthians 9:24 (NIV)

ELEVEN

I'm Running

> Let us throw off everything that hinders and the sin
> that so easily entangles, and let us run with
> perseverance the race marked out for us.
>
> HEBREWS 12:1 (NIV)

A Message from Tina

Anything worth having is worth fighting for. Any place worth going to is worth what it takes to get there. People who are running for all they're worth, who are fighting to maintain their relationship with God at any cost—those are the people I admire most. You know the shoppers who line up at Christmastime for whatever the toy is that every kid wants? I've never wanted any material thing enough to be in one of those lines. But I understand the kind of desire that says "I can't stand still. I've got to move toward what my heart longs for—and I won't stop until I reach it."

What about me? What do I want? I want God more than I want anything else. Way more. I can't just chill or stand still where my faith is concerned. I want more of God and so I'm running toward him. If God's desire is that I live a full, abundant life, then why would I choose anything over him? Why wouldn't I run after a good, loving God who has a plan for my life and can make everything in it—every relationship, every lesson, every trial, every accomplishment, and every sacrifice—more meaningful?

After all, my God is the one who lights my darkness, stills my storm, and brings hope out of my hopelessness. And every little bit I know of him makes me long to know him more. In him I have help, and hope, and joy. He decides how everything goes down. He calls the shots. He has the master plan. So whatever I've got to do to follow him, that's what I'll do.

"I'm Running" is definitely my favorite song to perform in concert. When I sing it I'm thinking, "God, I want you more than anything: more than riches, more than the praise of others, more than a happy family, or financial success, or fame." So I'm running. If I have to fall, I'll fall and get up again, but I'm running toward God with all my heart and all my strength. This life is a marathon, not a sprint—and I might not win the race, but I *will* finish. I don't know about you, but Tina's running. Whatever I've got to do, I'll do. He's just that good, and I love him that much.

be U!

Be full out and full on in your pursuit of God. Don't let anything get in the way of your relationship with him.

journal questions:

✳ Do you think of your life as a short race like a sprint, or as a long marathon?

_____

_____

_____

_____

_____

_____

_____

_____

✳ What does endurance mean to you?

_____

_____

_____

_____

_____

_____

_____

_____

✳ Is there anything you want enough to run toward it? Would you say you are running toward God right now, or away from him?

_____

_____

_____

_____

_____

_____

_____

_____

_____

_____

Those who hope in the LORD will renew their strength.

They will soar on wings like eagles; they will run and

not grow weary, they will walk and not be faint.

Isaiah 40:31 (NIV)

Gotta love somebody, touch somebody,

help somebody along the way.

—FROM "LOVE SOMEBODY"

In everything I showed you that by working

hard in this manner you must help the

weak and remember the words of the Lord

Jesus, that he himself said, "It is more

blessed to give than to receive."

Acts 20:35 (NASB)

TWELVE

Love Somebody

> Do nothing from selfishness or empty conceit, but with humility of mind regard one another as more important than yourselves; do not merely look out for your own personal interests, but also for the interests of others.
>
> PHILIPPIANS 2:3–4 (NASB)

A Message from Erica

Life is about making an impact, living on purpose, and letting God shine. Even when we didn't have enough ourselves, my mom always went out of her way to help other people. That was her way of letting God shine. I'll admit I didn't like her generosity much growing up, because sometimes there wasn't enough to go around for the eight siblings, cousins, and others in our own house. When you're young, sharing isn't always your number-one priority! But now that I'm an adult I'm proud of my mom, and of how she's always made an impact on those around her by giving. She's built a beautiful legacy, and it's one I hope to share.

Funny thing about helping others, though—you're just as blessed as they are by the giving. A few Christmases ago Tina and I went to an elementary school in Las Vegas and gave away winter coats. As we looked at all those adorable faces I thought of Jesus saying, "If you've done it unto the least of these, you've done it unto me." It was just the greatest feeling to share some of what we have with them. Another time we visited a women's shelter where the "gift" was just time, and a listening ear. We didn't sing, we didn't even talk—at least not that much! What we did was listen to the women's stories. No one there was saying "Feed me" or "pay my rent" or "buy me a car." What they were crying out for was someone to hold their hand, understand their heart, and let them know they were not alone. So if you think you can't give until you have something, or something more, you couldn't be more wrong. You have a heart to care. You have ears to hear. You have hands to reach out and touch.

I heard a story once about an old man whose wife died. A little neighbor boy wanted to do something, so he asked his mother if they could go to the old man's house. The mom took her son to the neighbor's house, and when they went inside the boy climbed up on the old man's lap and said, "I came to help you cry." Together, that's what they did. The boy knew that having someone to hold always helped when he needed to cry. So that's the kind of help he gave.

When my husband, Warryn, was in the hospital having surgery for kidney cancer, his mom brought a blank book to his room and encouraged everyone who visited to "write what you feel" in its pages. I don't think Warryn's made it through that book yet without crying, and neither have I. The presence of friends and their words of love and encouragement were just the kind of help he needed in a difficult time.

It's good to give money to a cause, or help build a house, or take a mission trip to a third world country. But you don't have to do any of that to help somebody. Remember, people don't care how much you know, they just wanna know how much you care. And you're never too young or too poor to show that you care.

be *U!*

This world has plenty of takers, and not enough givers. When God blesses you with more than you need, be a giver!

journal questions:

✳ How willing are you to help someone in need?

_____

_____

_____

_____

_____

_____

✳ How willing are you to receive help from others when *you* need it?

_____

_____

_____

_____

_____

_____

✳ How could you help someone in your family, your school, your neighborhood, or your church? What gifts do you have that you could share with others?

_____

_____

_____

_____

_____

_____

But whoever has the world's goods, and sees his brother

in need and closes his heart against him, how does the

love of God abide in him? Little children, let us not love

with word or with tongue, but in deed and truth.

1 John 3:17—18 (NASB)

77

be *strong*

It's all about accessorizing—right? The right pair of shoes,

a belt that pulls your outfit together, and maybe even a hat

that sets you apart from the others. That's what God's

talking about in Ephesians 6, when he tells us how to *be*

strong. But his armor is not intended to impress others; his

armor makes you strong. Strong in your convictions, strong

enough to do the right thing, strong enough to be the *you*

God created you to be.

Get up if you wanna get there—

clocks won't stop

and time won't wait.

—FROM "GET UP"

Be strong in the Lord

and in his mighty power.

Put on the full armor of God

so that you can take your stand

against the devil's schemes.

Ephesians 6:10—11 (NIV)

THIRTEEN

Get Up

Make every effort to add to your faith goodness;
and to goodness, knowledge; and to knowledge,
self-control; and to self-control, perseverance;
and to perseverance, godliness.

2 PETER 1:5–6 (NIV)

A Message from Tina

"Get Up" is the motivational anthem of the century for me! We could sit around forever shifting blame or making excuses about why we haven't done this, or that—but *we* are the ones responsible for our own lives. Most people don't want to hear that life is what you make it. They'd rather tell you a sad story about "shoulda, coulda, woulda." But others are willing to work: to put a plan in place and pursue it, knowing that they might have to fail a time or two on the way to winning. Which kind of person are you?

As people of faith, we should be the second kind. We have the Light of the World in our lives, and he should be our inspiration to "get up!" You (yes, you!) are one of God's greatest creations. You represent a mighty God who is your source of strength and hope. That should motivate you—I know it motivates me! Boxer Muhammed Ali used to say "I'm the greatest" to anyone who would listen. He believed it. He internalized it. He acted as if it were true. What if you and I acted as if we were great, too—not because of anything we've said or done, but because we were made in the image of a great and awesome God?

Even when I'm tired or things don't go my way, I'm motivated to "get up" because his greatness resides in me. Because I'm one of God's greatest creations, I've got things to do—and so do you! Maybe your community is counting on you to boost morale or help kids who need a hand or uplift people when they're down. Maybe you're made to design beautiful buildings or teach students or be writers who make sense of things for others—whatever it is, to do it, you've got to get up!

I don't want to be fifty or sixty years old and look up and think, *I haven't done anything.* There's no reason for that, because I've got time and opportunity, and I'm a child of God. You may not be famous, but you can make a big impact even as a student or a stay-at-home mom. In fact, loving, compassionate, responsible parenting is huge. Being a giver and not a taker is big! You don't need a lot of money to listen, or to love. Don't discredit your contribution, whatever it may be—and don't sell yourself short. Whatever it is you do, do the heck out of it. To whom much is given, much is required, so get up, girl—it's time for you to shine!

be U!

When God puts a dream in your heart, be ready to do your part to make it happen. Don't just wait for good things to come to you— get up!

journal questions:

✳ Take an inventory of your favorite excuses. Go ahead. Write 'em down. Now, which one of those "I can'ts" is bigger than God? (Hint: this list is gonna be shorter!)

_____

_____

_____

_____

_____

_____

_____

_____

_____

_____

* What would you try if you knew there was no way you could fail? Why not try it anyway?

_____

_____

_____

_____

_____

_____

_____

_____

✳ Do you have a dream that sounds too big to tell anyone about? Tell God about it, then ask him to help you get up and make it come true.

_____

_____

_____

_____

_____

_____

_____

_____

_____

Whatever you do, work at it with all your heart, as working for

the Lord, not for men, since you know that you will receive an

inheritance from the Lord as a reward.

Colossians 3:23—24 (NIV)

I don't know what to do but

what I do know—I trust you.

—FROM "I TRUST YOU"

In God I have put my trust, I shall not be

afraid. What can man do to me?

Psalm 56:11 (NASB)

F O U R T E E N

I Trust You

> Trust in the LORD with all your heart, and do not lean
> on your own understanding. In all your ways
> acknowledge him, and he will make your paths
> straight.
>
> PROVERBS 3:5–6 (NASB)

A Message from Erica

My husband Warryn and I have a different kind of love story. We met through music, through work, and so for a long time we were more like friends than anything else. I'd been through some bad relationships, and I'm not even sure I would have trusted him if he had come on really strong at first. I was engaged twice before and thought maybe I was destined to be "the girlfriend" but not "the wife," even though I wanted to be married. For years I had gone to everybody else for relationship answers—my girlfriends, my aunt, my youth pastor—but with Warryn I felt like God wanted me to ask *him* instead. When I felt the

Lord speak to me it was overwhelming. I prayed, "Lord, please let me know what you're doing in this one before my heart's all involved." I didn't want to mess up my life by marrying the wrong guy!

So we got married—we had a beautiful wedding. And we had a beautiful house and four cars and successful careers, so on the outside everything looked fantastic. But something was missing. I remember thinking, *I could leave this house for two months and I'm not sure he'd even notice.* A kind of "disconnect" was growing between us, and after our baby came it got even worse. (Those people who tell you a baby can "fix" what's broken in a relationship? They're kidding somebody.) I didn't want that kind of existence. I prayed, "Lord, if my husband loves me, let me feel it. Let me believe it. Please." The Lord answered my prayers. I realized that one of my problems was my own insecurities. I was attaching issues from previous relationships to my husband and blaming him for stuff he never did. On top of that, the enemy was trying to make me doubt what I knew God said. Needless to say, God fixed it!

Then when we were making *The Sound*, Warryn started feeling bad. I was leaving a day spa in L.A. and my phone rang. It was Warryn, and he said, "The doctor found something. A mass. On my kidney." I literally dropped to my knees right there. The people around me asked "Are you okay?" and I remember saying "No. But I will be." I went outside and walked down the sidewalk screaming for about a minute and a half. Then I called Tina and said, "Say something." She told me, "I know God to be a healer. You do, too. We saw that growing up. Hold on to it."

On the day that call came, and in the days afterward, I had to trust God in ways I'd never trusted him before. Exactly seven days after the doctors found Warryn's tumor, he had surgery to remove it. He spent seven hours in surgery, and another four in recovery. The songs from *The Sound* were going through my mind—"I Trust You" and "I'm Running." All I could say was, "Okay, God, I trust you. I don't know what to do, but I trust you." Warryn's surgery was 100 percent successful. His cancer is gone. No chemo. No radiation. Gone. We trusted God, and he helped us overcome a distant marriage, and then cancer. All we could do was bind together with each other and pray. But as we did we learned to put our personal things aside, and trust God to help us overcome. Today I have a strong, healthy husband, and we have a good marriage. I don't just sing the words "I Trust You"—I've lived them, and I'm going to keep on living them. What about you?

be U!

You've got a God who is worthy of your trust. Why don't you try him and see if he's true? You won't be disappointed. When you don't know what to do, be brave and put your trust in him.

journal questions:

✳ When is it easy for you to trust God? When is it hard?

_____

_____

_____

_____

_____

_____

✳ Who is the person you trust most in life? What about that person helps you to trust him or her?

_____

_____

_____

_____

_____

_____

_____

_____

✱ Are there things God has done for you in the past that have built your trust in him? Make a list of those things here.

_____

_____

_____

_____

_____

_____

_____

Though he slay me, yet will I hope in him.

Job 13:15 (NIV)

Champions never accept defeat;

they fall and get back on their feet. . . .

—FROM "DIRT"

I have told you these things, so that in me

you may have peace. In this world you will

have trouble, but take heart! I have

overcome the world.

John 16:33 (NIV)

FIFTEEN

Dirt

The God of all grace, who called you to his eternal
glory in Christ, after you have suffered a little while,
will himself restore you and make you strong.

1 PETER 5:10 (NIV)

A Message from Tina

A life is like a garden: It needs a little dirt to grow. Erica had the vision
for this song, and I love to sing it because I know it's true. Trees, roses,
all the beautiful things that bloom in a garden need their dirt to grow.
You and I need a little dirt, too. Ordinary, not-so-beautiful dirt is the
stuff that deepens our roots and keeps us reaching for the sky.

Think about it. We need resistance to grow strong. We need the
"dirt" of struggle or pressure to help us develop stamina and determination. Even if we'd rather skip them, we need the doubts, the short-
falls, and the roadblocks of life to motivate us, because what we have to

work for we tend to appreciate more. I feel bad for kids who grow up having everything they want or need placed in their lap. When good stuff comes to us with ease, we can't really understand the value of it—but if we work hard for something we *know* what it costs. My oldest child takes great pride in earning things. She works for the things she wants, and that work is not just getting her a hoped-for reward; it's growing and shaping her character.

Beauty can bloom from unwanted or unplanned trials, too. I did not want my youngest child to be born prematurely, but she came at thirty-three weeks and weighed just three pounds at birth. I could hold her in one hand! I thought, *Lord, this is my baby. I want to cradle her and feed her and keep her safe, but she has to stay in this nursery and struggle to get strong.* So I went home, and she stayed in the hospital— and let me tell you that was one crazy situation. She was surrounded by doctors and nurses and machines, and I was helpless to do anything for her. But through that "dirt," my prayer life bloomed! I learned how to rely and depend on God in a very difficult situation. The doctors were doing their best, but they were only "practicing" medicine on my baby girl while God was executing her healing. She was there for a month, and I prayed about every little thing while she grew strong enough to come home. Today, she is the fieriest child ever! She keeps me on my toes, my Meela, and what we struggled through makes me appreciate her strong temperament even more.

Has life thrown some dirt on you? Get your spirit right. Learn to lean on God for peace in the midst of your storm. Imagine the garden God is nurturing as you struggle, and remember: we all need a little dirt to grow!

be *U!*

When life deals you a difficult situation, ask God to use it to help you grow, then be patient as he makes something beautiful from your "dirt."

journal questions:

✳ How do you respond when suffering through hard times?

_____

_____

_____

_____

_____

_____

_____

_____

_____

_____

✳ Can you think of some "dirt" from the past that has helped you to grow?

_____

_____

_____

_____

_____

_____

_____

_____

_____

✳ What "dirty situation" are you facing right now? Ask God to use it to help you grow, then watch what happens!

I consider that our present sufferings are not worth

comparing with the glory that will be revealed in us.

Romans 8:18 (NIV)

The past has passed away,

finally I have forgiven me.

—FROM "FORGIVEN ME"

Then Peter came and said to him, "Lord,

how often shall my brother sin against me

and I forgive him? Up to seven times?"

Jesus said to him, "I do not say to you, up to

seven times, but up to seventy times seven."

Matthew 18:21—22 (NASB)

SIXTEEN

Forgiven Me

> For this reason I say to you, her sins, which are
> many, have been forgiven, for she loved much; but
> he who is forgiven little, loves little. Then he said to
> her, "Your sins have been forgiven."
>
> LUKE 7:47–48 (NASB)

A Message from Tina

"Forgiven Me" is my theme song. It really is! I'm harder on myself than I could ever be on others and I need a lot of forgiveness—so I've got to constantly remember that when I confess, God forgives. If I've hurt someone, broken someone's heart, made a bad decision, failed to keep a promise—I'm always sick about it. I can beat myself up for a long time over a mistake I've made, so I have to keep preaching to myself "Tina, God forgave that one. *Let it go.*"

Of course, whatever I can "naturally" remedy, I do—apologizing, confessing to the person I've wounded—but there's a part of the forgiveness equation that only God can do. And I'm so thankful that he's faithful to forgive when I come up short. God says we're to forgive others "seventy times seven"—in the same generous, not-keeping-score kind of way. But too many times we say we believe *God* forgave us, and then we refuse to forgive ourselves! Do you see how wrong that is? Listen—if God can forgive me, then I *must* forgive myself. I can't keep dragging up the past. If I truly believe the Word of God—which says, "There is no condemnation for those who are in Christ Jesus" (Romans 8:1 NIV)—and if you are "in Christ Jesus," then you are cool.

You know what happens when we hold on to old sin? We convince ourselves that we deserve to live a miserable life—that no one's going to love us, that nothing's going to go our way, and that God will never bless us again. You see what's wrong with that kind of attitude, don't you? It completely counts out God's grace! Sure—it's good to claim your mistake. Own it. Say "Yes, I did that. I committed the crime. I told the lie. I hurt innocent people. I hurt myself." Then, do what Jesus told the woman caught in adultery—the one caught in broad daylight and dragged out onto the street to be stoned for her sin—to do. *Go and sin no more.* And then agree with God and forgive yourself.

You don't live in a time machine. You can't go back and undo what is done. You can impact your future, but not your past. So stop blaming yourself. Stop hanging your head in shame. Instead, celebrate what God has done for you, and decide to live each day in a "forgiven" way that will honor him. Leave your old, forgiven sin with him, and move on. He will cause all things to work for your good and his glory, and you'll be able to say, "I've forgiven me."

be *U!*

You are precious in God's sight, and your sins are forgiven when you confess them to God. Be the free, forgiven girl that you are in Christ. Don't let memories of the past drag you down.

journal questions:

✳ Is there something you've confessed to God and received his forgiveness for, but can't seem to forget?

_____

_____

_____

_____

_____

_____

_____

_____

_____

_____

❋ Are you a wiser judge than God? If he's forgiven you, what keeps you from forgiving yourself?

_____

_____

_____

_____

_____

_____

_____

_____

_____

_____

* Imagine leaving an "old sin" behind once and for all. How would it feel to let go of the regret and shame of that mistake?

_____

_____

_____

_____

_____

_____

_____

_____

_____

If you, LORD, should mark iniquities, O Lord, who could stand?

But there is forgiveness with you, that you may be feared.

Psalm 130:3—4 (NASB)

PART FIVE

be *you*

It's no fun to live your life pretending to be something

you're not. If you're always putting on an act, you'll never

be sure of what you've got. It's better to be 100 percent

you than an imitation of anybody else (even a good one!).

God knew what he was doing when he made you, and he

doesn't make mistakes. Take the time to discover your gifts,

your heart's desires, your dreams and goals. Then be fully,

completely, gratefully, and joyfully . . . you.

Friends with limited warranties,

until you I never knew a

lifetime-guaranteed friend

could be my reality.

—FROM "WHAT A FRIEND"

Greater love has no one than this, that

someone lay down his life for his friends.

John 15:13 (ESV)

SEVENTEEN

What a Friend

No longer do I call you servants, for the servant does not know what his master is doing; but I have called you friends, for all that I have heard from my Father I have made known to you.

JOHN 15:15 (ESV)

A Message from Erica

I was a sweet, emotional kid—the kind of kid who would cry and praise God in church like I had been through the storm, like I knew what tough times were all about. I loved hearing about the cross, about the woman at the well, the Good Samaritan, and especially the story of Joseph. The stories were beautiful, but back then I didn't really understand the cost of redemption. I loved Jesus and I wanted to know him, but I hadn't experienced enough of life yet to grasp the awesomeness of God's grace.

The songs I sang in church were dear to me in childhood, but their meaning became so much richer as I grew up. When you take a few bad turns you learn what repentance means, and in those grown-up moments of repentance I came to know the power and presence of God in a deeply personal way. To this day I marvel at the overwhelming truth that he loves me enough to *visit* me. A personal visit from Jesus—are you kidding me? It's crazy (in a good way). I am the recipient of his perfect love and he is my friend like no other.

I grew up with so many great friends. Tina and I were both blessed with kind, loving, understanding, encouraging friends. But God is the most incredible friend I have ever had, or ever will. He's seen the very worst of Erica—and he's kept on loving me, even when I mess up or fail him. One day I will see him, and when I do we will not be strangers because I have come to know him through his son, who loved me and gave himself up for me. He's exactly the kind of friend I'd like to be: faithful, true, always loving, always forgiving, and always encouraging me to be what he knows I can be.

Maybe you think that God can't be a friend to you because you're not deserving of him. Maybe you're saying to yourself, *Sure, that friend thing works for her—but she hasn't done what I've done.* Listen: God still loves you. He still cares. He is still all about lifting, restoring, repairing, renewing, and reviving. And not just for other people. For *you.* He's that kind of friend—today, tomorrow, and forever. What a friend!

be U!

Be the kind of friend you need. Is there someone in your school or neighborhood that needs a friend? WWJD?

journal questions:

❋ What kind of grade would you give yourself as a friend? What one thing could make you a better friend to others?

_____

_____

_____

_____

_____

_____

_____

_____

_____

_____

✳ Describe the perfect friend. What attributes would he or she have? Which of these describe you?

_____

_____

_____

_____

_____

_____

_____

✳ What does it mean to you to call yourself a friend of God?

_____

_____

_____

_____

_____

_____

_____

_____

✳ What does it mean to you to call God *your* friend?

_____

_____

_____

_____

_____

_____

_____

A friend loves at all times, and a brother is

born for adversity.

Proverbs 17:17 (ESV)

I'm just ordinary people,

who found extraordinary love. . . .

—FROM "ORDINARY PEOPLE"

Listen, my beloved brothers, has not God

chosen those who are poor in the world to be

rich in faith and heirs of the kingdom, which

he has promised to those who love him?

James 2:5 (ESV)

EIGHTEEN

Ordinary People

What no eye has seen, nor ear heard, nor the heart of man imagined, what God has prepared for those who love him.

1 CORINTHIANS 2:9 (ESV)

A Message from Erica

Sometimes people confuse being in the limelight with being something special. Believe me when I say they're not the same. Those people you see in the limelight—up front, bigger than life—they're no better than you or me. In fact, you'd be surprised to find that they've got their share of issues and insecurities, too.

Growing up, I was "little Erica"—the lead singer in my church. I believed I had friends because I sang and was accepted because I sang, but I wished I could sing better. I had a solid core group of friends, but even though I was in the spotlight a little, I knew I wasn't the cutest one or the one with the best clothes. We didn't have a lot of money back then. In a house full of sisters, my clothes were mostly hand-me-downs. Those things can play games with your confidence, but now I see that what I believed to be disadvantages were the very things that built my character!

I may be on stage singing in front of a crowd, but I'm proud to say that I'm just Erica—an ordinary person with an extraordinary God.

Ordinary people can shine. Don't believe me? Like the song says, "God took ordinary me and gave me a chance." I might have seen "only average" when I looked in the mirror, but God saw a gift that he planned to use. When I realized whose I am, and that he's chosen me— I've got all the advantage I need. It's God's opinion of me that matters most, and he tells me in his word that he has loved me with an ever-lasting love, and that he will never leave me or forsake me. How great is that?

With God's love and presence, you can give the devil a black eye when he tries to shake your confidence or make you doubt that you are special in God's eyes. When those feelings of insecurity come up (and they will!), just say, "I've dealt with this before. God is for me. He makes my ordinary stuff extraordinary. He's that big."

So trust me. God loves ordinary you. There's something special about you that nobody else in this world has. The key is, you have to cultivate it! The gifts you have point to the purpose you're made for. I'm excited to see where Mary Mary will take me, and how God will use ordinary me. But I'm just as thrilled to imagine what he'll do with ordinary you!

be U!

Be thankful for the extraordinary love God has shown you, and be ready to give him praise when he causes you to shine!

journal questions:

✳ When do you feel ordinary? Extraordinary?

_____

_____

_____

_____

_____

_____

_____

_____

_____

_____

✳ Is there an "ordinary" person you know who shines? Describe that person.

_____

_____

_____

_____

_____

_____

_____

_____

_____

_____

_____

✳ Who do you look up to? Who do you know that looks up to you?

_____

_____

_____

_____

_____

_____

_____

_____

_____

Humble yourselves, therefore, under the mighty hand

of God so that at the proper time he may exalt you.

1 Peter 5:6 (ESV)

You think I'm so fresh . . .

You think I'm so sweet,

it's the God in me . . .

—FROM "GOD IN ME"

To them God chose to make known how

great . . . are the riches of the glory of this

mystery, which is *Christ in you,* the hope of

glory.

Colossians 1:27 (ESV)

NINETEEN

God in Me

I have been crucified with Christ. It is no longer I who
live, but Christ who lives in me.

GALATIANS 2:20 (ESV)

A Message from Tina

You know those people, right? Everybody wants to see what they're wearing, what they're driving, what their take on things is. They've got it goin' on. They're strong. Powerful. Big in the room. The lyric for *God in Me* begins, "You're so fly, you're so high, everybody around you trying to figure out why. . . ."

This world is filled with people who draw others like a magnet—and it seems like it's their exterior we're drawn to. But the truth is, the really powerful people have more than that. They've got a presence that's out of this world. They're at peace. Confident. Joyful.

Jesus was like that. People wanted to be where he was. I don't think you can get any more popular than Jesus. They followed him. Listened to him. Pressed in on him. He had that thing I call "the God factor."

People who love him have it, too.

In these times when the economy is bad, people are losing jobs, losing houses—you might think being joyful is impossible. But it's not. When I see people with that calm, that confidence—I say it's the God in them. The God factor. And I want to be near them, to know what they know and have what they have. Not the material stuff, though. The peace.

It's not clothes, cars, where you live, or where your kids go to school that makes you stand out. It's the God in you. That glow, that light, that swagger and sureness only comes when you've got God in your life, and you're hitting the floor on a regular basis, taking your strength and your direction from him.

Listen, I know my weaknesses. But because I've got a heart for God, he lets my light shine. I'm floored by that. Anything good in me you see is not Tina—it's the God in me. It's not about me getting on a bullhorn. It's about getting on my knees, in private, and saying, "God, I wanna be like you. Be big in my life."

I'll tell you who has what I'm talking about. My uncle Charles has it. He's just an unassuming man from Texarkana, Arkansas, and yet he's so wise and full of God that everybody loves him. Uncle Charles was my pastor growing up—a simple yet powerful man. Even today, when I come into his church I feel the power of God. He may not be the most famous or the most powerful preacher in L.A., but the God in him really shines.

So believe me: it's the God in you that will make you stand out. It's the God in you that will make people want to know you and be around you. Be honest about your flaws, and be confident in who God is. Let him be that "signature" thing about you. Be content in who he's made you to be, and don't always be clamoring for more of this, or more of that. Don't wish for somebody else's gift. Learn to celebrate the God in you, girl.

You'll be glad you did.

be *U!*

You're one of a kind—unique. Don't dress up the outside and forget who lives in you. Be content. Be confident. Be grateful for the God in you.

journal questions:

❋ Is there someone you wish you could be more like? What qualities in them are you attracted to?

_____

_____

_____

_____

_____

_____

✳ Do you think others might see "the God in you"? Why or why not?

_____

_____

_____

_____

_____

✳ If you could ask God to give you more of "something special," what would that something be?

_____

_____

_____

_____

_____

_____

✳ Ask someone who knows you well (and loves you enough to tell the truth!) to describe the good things they see in you. What did they say? Do any of the things they see sound like God things?

_____

_____

_____

_____

_____

You should clothe yourselves instead with the beauty that

comes from within, the unfading beauty of a gentle and

quiet spirit, which is so precious to God.

1 Peter 3:4 (NLT)

123

He's something like the best of them,

He's nothing like the rest of them.

—FROM "SUPERFRIEND"

A man of too many friends comes to ruin,

But there is a friend who sticks closer than

a brother.

Proverbs 18:24 (NASB)

TWENTY

Superfriend

Greater love has no one than this, that one lay down his life for his friends.

JOHN 15:13 (NASB)

A Message from Tina

Friends are a big deal for Erica and me. We have a group called the "Gs" that are our lifetime friends, and I can't begin to tell you all the stuff we've been through together. We still see each other whenever we can, even though we live in different cities and our lives are all super busy. I've had and lost friends in my life, but thank God this group is tight. Each of us has played a role in the Gs: the peacemaker, the troublemaker, the talker, the sensitive one—and although those roles have changed as we've grown, the love we have for each other has not. This is the group that used to pitch in two bucks apiece so we could all go to the mall together. The group that had taco parties with just the basics: meat, shell, and cheese.

Through it all we've stuck together. We've experienced marriages, children, divorces, and interventions. It hasn't always been pretty—but it *has* always been real. If you asked any one of us if the others "had our back," she would answer "yes" without even thinking about it. I remember a long time ago this cute new guy came into our church. All ten of us noticed him—and three of the Gs liked him—a lot. But you know what? We didn't compete with one another for his attention. We talked about it together and decided, "It's not on us. It's on him. We're not pressing." Another time one of the Gs connected with an old boyfriend of mine from high school. Even though it was years later, she asked if I was okay with it (I was). But she still asked. There have even been times when all we could say to each other was "Pray for me—I've gotta do this one by myself." You better believe we did.

A lot of people don't honor friendship that way—but we're serious about it. We put time together on our calendars, because if we didn't it might not happen. Sure, it takes effort. But it is so, so worth it. You know that saying "No man is an island"? Believe it. Go to the trouble it takes to keep your friendships healthy and strong. Take the time to at least try to get it right. I keep my friends close. We all should. But there is a friend that is closer than a brother, and that friend is God. He is the original superfriend. He's the best. He is never forcing, never judging, gentle, loving, and wise. He's always on our side. He always has our back. He's the one. He's my superfriend, and he can be yours, too!

be *U!*

Jesus *is* a superfriend, and he wants to be that kind of friend to you. All you have to do is say yes, and become a friend to the one who's already a friend to you!

journal questions:

❋ Have you ever been betrayed by a friend? What does it mean to you to know that there is a superfriend who has promised to never, ever leave you or forsake you?

_____

_____

_____

_____

_____

_____

_____

_____

_____

_____

_____

✳ Superfriends bring peace and not chaos to their relationships, just like Jesus did. Are you a superfriend, or a so-so friend?

_____

_____

_____

_____

_____

_____

_____

_____

_____

✳ Think of your very best friend. What do you love most about him or her? Would you give your life for them? That's what Jesus did for you!

_____

_____

_____

_____

_____

_____

_____

_____

_____

Beloved, if God so loved us, we also ought to love

one another.

1 John 4:11 (NASB)

When I think about all

my blessings, oh I'm telling you—

God's been good to me!

—FROM "GOOD TO ME"

The lines have fallen to me in pleasant

places; indeed, my heritage is beautiful

to me.

Psalm 16:6 (NASB)

TWENTY - ONE

Good to Me

How great is your goodness, which you have stored
up for those who fear you, which you have wrought
for those who take refuge in you.

PSALM 31:19 (NASB)

A Message from Erica

I love what this song says. Tina started singing the melody to me and
we wrote the hook in the office. Then we went into the studio and my
husband Warryn did the track. When we finished it, Destiny's Child—
back when there were four of them—was making a record, so we re-
corded it with them. To me, it's a song about misconceptions and truth.
The misconception is that we often judge people by what we see, and
only what we see. The truth is that God is at work even when we can't
recognize his actions on our behalf.

When people look at Tina and me as Mary Mary, they assume they know what our life has been like. They don't. It hasn't always been easy. It hasn't always been fun. We had our share of struggles growing up, and we've even struggled our own fair share as grown-ups. They might imagine we've never had a down day between us, but the truth is we've had plenty.

The song talks about hand-me-downs and sharing stuff—and that's not pretend. That's real. I remember we used to have the grossest little orange car. I'm not kidding. It was ridiculous. Used. Just awful. We used to drive around in that car and duck—praying that none of our friends would see it. We'd go to church, go to sing, go everywhere in that little orange car. When I look back on it now, I don't just remember how embarrassed I was about the car. I remember how good God was to give it to us! We had transportation—even if it wasn't pretty. We didn't have to walk or ride the bus (even if we did have to duck!).

Listen—no matter what your past holds, I'm sure that God's been good to you, too. How do I know? Not because I know your story—I don't. I know he's been good because I know *him.* He's loving. He's faithful. He's kind. He's forgiving. He's able to save us and keep us. If you don't see it now, I hope you will. Maybe one day soon you'll read something, hear something, meet a person, hear a song, and you'll realize that God's been good to you all along.

be *U!*

Your relationship with God is the most important one you will ever have. His goodness to you is a fact. Be aware of the ways he blesses you, and be willing to share his love with others in your life. You are his child. You are loved. Be satisfied in him.

journal questions:

✳ How has God been good to you?

_____

_____

_____

_____

_____

✳ Can you see how God may have used hard or unpleasant things in your life to shape your character or to make you stronger?

_____

_____

_____

_____

_____

_____

_____

_____

* What words would you choose to describe God? Why did you select the words you did?

_____

_____

_____

_____

_____

_____

_____

✳ Describe a situation from your past where God took good care of you, maybe without you even realizing it. What did he do?

_____

_____

_____

_____

_____

_____

We know that God causes all things to work together for good to

those who love God, to those who are called according to his

purpose. For I am convinced that neither death, nor life, nor angels,

nor principalities, nor things present, nor things to come, nor powers,

nor height, nor depth, nor any other created thing, will be able to

separate us from the love of God, which is in Christ Jesus our Lord.

Romans 8:28, 38—39 (NASB)

Q&A with Erica and Tina

1. Who is Tina Campbell? Who is Erica Campbell? Describe yourself in a few words:

Erica says: I am an open-hearted, free-spirited person and very loving but laid back. I think I may be Jamaican—no worries man!

Tina says: I am a loving firecracker who's super honest, and she's often misunderstood cuz she's feisty—but she has a great heart! We're a perfect pair!

2. Who or what were your greatest influences growing up?

Tina says: My big brother Darrel and my dad were big influences because they always seemed fearless. They both acted as if they owned the world. I always admired that. My mom and her big heart 'ole heart of gold was a huge influence. And my uncle Charles and his "don't really wanna be bothered but will help anybody who really needs it" type personality definitely was a big influence.

Erica says: I had the coolest big cousin named Barbette—she's beautiful She could sing when I was younger, and she always had cute boyfriends! Shallow but true ☺. My big sister Maliea is another one, I love her. I watched and listened to her more than she knows.

3. Do you have heroes? Who are they?

Erica says: My mom. She's simply incredible. She should write a book because her whole life has been one amazing journey—the good, the bad, and the ugly. She's *never* taken her eyes off God, *ever* . . . And Oprah, of course, she's amazing!

Tina says: My mom is definitely my hero. She's sweet, honest, fair, compassionate, free-spirited, considerate, peaceful, joyful . . . oh, and she raised all nine of us plus extra relatives with no money. She never went to the spa, took a private vacation, had a baby sitter or nanny, and she never complained. She's a superhero!!! And, of course, Oprah! She does it all.

4. In what ways did you struggle to "become you"? What forces worked against you and what helped you to become authentic and real?

Tina says: I'm quite the critical person. I'm also a bit of a perfectionist, so I was always the victim of my own critiques, which meant I always thought everything about me or whatever I'd do could've been so much better. It was probably a few years past eighteen when I realized, *I am what I am.* My flaws, strengths, mistakes, achievements, whatever it is, good or bad, that I like or dislike about myself, don't negate the fact that I'm *still me*. So once I realized that I may not ever measure up to someone I really admired or to some mythical, perfect being, 'cause ain't nobody perfect but Jesus, all I could do was work on being my best self. That's when I found Tina! I realized I may forever be a work in progress. God ain't through with me yet, but I alone, in my own special way, have something special to offer the world, and that became my focus.

Erica says: Giiirl! I struggled like you wouldn't believe! I didn't really gain confidence until I was in my twenties. From not liking my voice, to my hair, my weight, my nose! You name it, the enemy had his way with my head! But I have come to realize how *fabulous* I am, and I'm not ashamed to say it! I rock! There are so many negatives to fight; I need to be *my own* biggest cheerleader—no boyfriend or husband or bff needs to validate me. After years of the ultimate pity-party, I just got over it and realized God don't make no junk!

5. What would you say to a young girl who's in the process of becoming who God made her to be? How would you encourage her? Warn her? Advise her?

Erica says: To any young woman "becoming," I would say relax; all things come in God's time! We all need a 'lil dirt to grow, so take every challenge head on and fight it. With God all things are possible! Don't waste time waiting on the day you "become" who you should be! Celebrate yourself in the process; you'll never get this time back! Believe God has you right where you should be! Laugh, dance, smile.

Tina says: Erica said it best. There's no more to add.

6. What do you pray for your daughters?

Tina says: I pray that the blood of Jesus would cover my children wherever they go to keep them from harm and danger. I pray that God would guard them naturally and spiritually from things that would come to destroy their innocence and defile their youth. I pray that they'd do well in school and have happy and healthy relationships in childhood through adulthood. I pray that they'd be filled with love and joy, that they'd be considerate and compassionate, respectful and responsible, confident and productive. I pray that God would reveal himself and his amazing love to them individually so they'll have their own personal relationship with him. I pray they be bold witnesses for Jesus and declare his kingdom to the world. I pray that God would use their gifts and talent for his glory. I pray that God would cause them to reach their fullest potential in every area of their existence. And finally, that God's perfect will would be manifested in their lives.

Erica says: Wow! That she has a strong desire to serve and please the Lord with her life. That she loves the Word of God. That she lives and loves freely; that she's smart and honest; caring yet strong; and loving, with compassion for people. That she won't be afraid of anything! That she will have awesome friends and a family of her own one day! I pray all God's best for Krista Nicole.

7. Why do you sing?

Erica says: I sing because I'm happy, LOL! No, really, I do! Music, in and of itself, an awesome song, a lyric, or just beautifully played instruments just move me. And to be able to communicate so many emotions with a song, my song, is a gift! I love to sing!!

Tina says: I have to echo Erica. It makes me feel good when I sing. It makes me smile, it makes me dream. It gives me an escape from what may not be a good day or circumstance. Plus, I know I have a God-given gift, and I'm grateful for that. I'd do it if there was no record deal, no stage, no sound system, no attention whatsoever. I'd do it for free with a fork in my hand as my mic, in front of my bathroom mirror, loud and strong just for me. I absolutely love it. It makes me happy.

8. Did you ever wish to be something different than what you are?

Tina says: I thought I'd be a music teacher, perhaps a make-up artist. Never saw myself in this place, but I know I'm called to be here. And I actually love it. I'm honored God chose me.

Erica says: I can truly say I've always wanted to sing my whole life, I feel so blessed to have the career/ministry that I have. I love being able to share my music with the world—to have your voice heard is incredible!

9. Was there a time when you questioned God? What was the outcome?

Erica says: Of course! We always have questions; I think questions are healthy. And with every question there is an answer. God has never failed me. Things don't always work out how I'd like them to, but I believe all things work together for the good of them that love the Lord, so I just remind myself who my God is and chill! He's always replaced my doubt with his awesomeness!

Tina says: After becoming an adult, I questioned whether God was actually mine and would listen to me and talk to me. I kinda felt like I always need my pastor, my parents, or people I respected in the faith to connect me to or receive a word from God. It frustrated me and made me question the authenticity of what I had been taught and raised to believe. So I started praying simple prayers and asking God to answer them if he was really real and could really hear me. Nobody knew my requests. It was just between me and God. When these simple prayers were answered, I found the scripture that says "Ask and it shall be given, seek and ye shall find, knock and the door will be open unto you" to be real and true.

10. Describe a time when you trusted God beyond what you could see. What was the outcome?

Tina says: When my daughter Meela was being born prematurely, I prayed with great expectation that God would let her come out fully developed, with healthy organs, with all the activities of her limbs, and no other health deficiencies. Although she was born at three pounds and she didn't come home for three and a half weeks, she was the picture of health. And there were many kids in her same scenario that were not as healthy. I believe that was God answering my prayers specifically 'cause I expected him to.

Erica says: This may seem small to some, but when I was about eighteen years old I wanted to go to a COGIC (Church of God in Christ) convention. I had a job, I payed tithes, and I gave offering; so when I need extra spending cash, I prayed that God would send a special blessing my way. I truly believed he would. A week went by, and I started packing for my trip, and I went to a small inexpensive store. While there, I saw a brother from my church, and he said, "I see how you are faithful to God and the church and just wanted to bless you with a hundred dollars." That was amazing to me at that age! I trusted God, I asked, and he answered! I'll never forget that it wasn't the money that was a big deal, God actually answered *me*!

11. What's your favorite song to sing?

Erica says: "Goodness Mercy and Grace" by the Winans.

Tina says: Right now, it's Israel Haughton's "Goodness and Mercy" and Michael Jackson's "Off the Wall."

12. What is your vision or hope for "Be You"?

Erica says: Our vision for this book is that it would open the eyes of young people and give them insight on how to live joyful, peaceful, successful, abundant overcoming realistic victorious *Christian* lives!

Tina says: Once again, I concur. Erica said it best.

13. Do you have a favorite Bible verse? If so, what is it?

Tina says: Jeremiah 32:17 reminds me that everything is possible when I put my faith in the Almighty God.

Erica says: My favorite Bible verse is Proverbs 3:5–6. I love this verse, and I trust God—period.

About the Authors

Growing up as sisters in a large family in Inglewood, California, Erica and Tina Campbell first sang publicly in the local church choir and received their first break in 1998 with a song on the *Prince of Egypt* soundtrack. Now, they are three-time Grammy winners—their most recent being their 2009 win for Best Gospel Performance for their hit single "Get Up." They are also Dove, Stellar, MOBO, and American Music Award winners. Their group name was inspired by the two Marys in the Bible—Mary, the mother of Jesus, and Mary Magdalene. Mary Mary wants their duo name to communicate that God's love is extended to all. This R&B, urban gospel duo performs for audiences of thousands across the country.